Copyright © 2025 Bright Ed Up LLC All rights reserved. Except as permitted under the U.S. Copyright Act of 1976, no part of this publication can be reproduced, distributed, or transmitted in any form or by any means, without the prior consent except in the case of brief quotations embodied in critical reviews and certain other noncommercial uses permitted by copyright law. For permission requests, contact the author at: seungkataii@gmail.com Printed in the United States of America

Version_1

PREFACE

Growing up in the United States, the Temple was at the heart of my family's life. While celebrating the many Lao festivals, I often found myself lost in translation. The monks chanted in an ancient language that most Lao people never understood. Kneeling for long periods brought aches, and the rituals, while beautiful, felt more like cultural tradition than a spiritual journey towards self-awakening.

One cherished memory stands out— Tahk Baht (giving alms). We filled the monks' offering bowls with snacks, candy, fruit, rice, kao thom and donate the cash. Later, temple volunteers would redistribute these offerings, and as children, we eagerly scrambled for the candy. Reflecting on those moments, it's bittersweet to see that for many kids today, candy remains the highlight of temple visits. Yet, through the years, my curiosity about the teachings and rituals never faded.

I was fortunate to have a mentor - my father. A former Theravada Buddhist monk, historian, educator and freedom fighter was one of the few who possessed rare knowledge of Buddhism and its profound connection to Lao culture. "it is inseparable" he often said. Men like my father, honored with the title "Maha" meaning "Great One," were rare custodians of this knowledge. Today, there are fewer and fewer of them left, especially abroad.

From ages eleven to thirteen, my summers were spent at the temple, ordained as a novice monk or Jua. This rite of passage, bringing great merit to my parents, introduced me to Buddhist life. I learned a few basic chants but rarely grasped their meanings. Those summers were less about spiritual growth and more about keeping young boys busy and out of trouble. Without understanding the language of Buddhism, we often misinterpret its essence of looking inward and striving for personal insight and spiritual growth. Rather, we often mistakenly attribute supernatural powers connecting them to the will of spirits and deities influenced by ancient practices of Animism and Brahmanism predating Buddhism in Laos.

Buddhism, at its core, offers ethical guidelines, philosophical insights, and meditative practices designed to deepen understanding, cultivate mindfulness, and foster compassion. At the age of twenty-five after graduating college, I was ordained as a monk or kuba. Becoming a monk is one of the highest merit one can give to his parents – a gesture of great gratitude. What began as a plan for a two-week stay turned into one rainy season completing one Phansa. During that time, I learned meditation, recited Theravada Buddhist verses, taught myself basic Lao, and developed a deeper interest in the Buddha's teachings. For a time, I felt I could follow in my father's footsteps and remain a monk for many years. However, life as a layman eventually took over—work, further education, and later, marriage. Even so, my journey in Buddhism continues, enriched by life's milestones.

It has been 50 years since the Lao diaspora began, following the civil war that led to the fall of the Royal Lao Government and the establishment of the Lao People's Democratic Republic. Many Lao refugees resettled in English-speaking countries such as the United States, Canada, Australia, the United Kingdom, and New Zealand, bringing with them a rich heritage of culture, cuisine, and the profound traditions of Theravada Buddhism.

The resettlement process came with challenges: cultural adjustments, economic struggles, racism, discrimination, mental health concerns, and educational barriers. Today, many younger-generation Lao Americans do not speak the Lao language or fully understand the traditions and practices of Lao Theravada Buddhism. This guide seeks to bridge that gap—to inspire learning, curiosity, respect, and pride in these ancestral traditions. May it serve as a companion for those seeking spiritual growth while preserving the essence of Theravada Buddhism for generations to come.

Thank you for your endearing support. – Seung Kataii

TABLE OF CONTENTS

1. Introduction to Buddhism — Page 6
2. Theravada Buddhism — Page 6
3. The Importance of Buddhism in Lao Culture — Page 7
4. The Four Noble Truths — Page 8
5. The Eightfold Path — Page 10
6. The Five Precepts — Page 11
7. The Triple Gem — Page 13
8. The Beginning of Theravada Buddhism in Laos — Page 13
9. Lao Culture and Festivals we Celebrate — Page 14
10. Basic Chanting and its Meaning — Page 26
11. Incorporating Buddhism into Daily Life — Page 40
12. Pronunciation of Pāli-English Text — Page 44
13. Glossary — Page 48
14. Annual Festival Calendar — Page 47
15. References — Page 49
16. Afterword — Page 50
17. Acknowledgments — Page 51

Introduction to Buddhism

Buddhism, understood today as both a religion and philosophy, was founded by Siddhartha Gautama "the Buddha" more than 2,600 years ago in the region of modern-day India. Scholars consider Buddhism one of the major world religions, with about 500 million followers. Its practice has historically been most prominent in East, South, and Southeast Asia. The Buddha discovered the cause of suffering, craving, and the way to end it. Through this understanding, he attained enlightenment, completely removing the roots of greed, hatred, and delusion from his mind. He taught these truths to the world. By practicing his teachings, mankind can completely end suffering in their lives.

What is Theravada Buddhism

Theravada Buddhism, meaning 'the doctrine of the elders,' is one of the oldest forms of Buddhism. It emphasizes the teachings of the Buddha as preserved in the Pali Canon, a collection of ancient scriptures. This tradition is considered by many to be the closest to the original teachings of the Buddha. Theravada Buddhism focuses on the individual's path to enlightenment through personal effort and adherence to the Buddha's teachings. The ultimate goal is to become an Arahant, a person who has achieved enlightenment and liberation from the cycle of birth, death, and rebirth. This practice is predominant in Laos, Thailand, Cambodia, Myanmar, and Sri Lanka.

The Importance of Buddhism in Lao Culture

Buddhism is deeply intertwined with Lao culture and daily life. It is not just a religion but a way of life that influences various aspects of Lao society. The teachings of the Buddha provide moral guidance and a framework for living a compassionate and mindful life. Festivals and ceremonies are integral to Lao people, serving as important spiritual milestones throughout the year. These events, such as Boun Pha Vaehd, Boun Khao Phansa, and Boun Bee Mai Lao (Lao New Year), bring communities together in celebration, reflection, and merit-making. They offer opportunities to honor heritage, practice faith, and strengthen communal bonds. Through these traditions, Buddhism continues to play a vital role in preserving Lao cultural identity and fostering a sense of unity and continuity among its people worldwide.

Buddhism has many sects, but the three largest are:

- **Theravada Buddhism** (The School of the Elders)
- **Mahayana Buddhism** (The Great Vehicle)
- **Vajrayana Buddhism** (The Way of the Diamond)

Each sect has diverse traditions, but these are the fundamental beliefs shared across most sects:

1. **No-self (Annata):** All Buddhists agree that the self is an illusion. There is no permanent "me." Instead, Buddhism recognizes impermanence and interconnectedness.

2. **Impermanence (Anicca):** Buddhists believe that everything is transient. Everything changes; nothing remains the same forever, including our thoughts, feelings, and physical existence.

3. **Karma:** The law of moral causation, you create it and experience it. Actions have consequences, and our intentions shape our future experiences. Good actions can lead to good results, and bad actions can lead to bad results.

4. **The Four Noble Truths:** These truths form the foundation of Buddhism:
   1. **The Truth of Suffering (Dukkha):**

      What it means: Life is full of ups and downs because we are emotional beings with feelings. It's not always fun, happy, or perfect. At times, we may feel emotions like anger, disappointment, fear, sadness, or hurt.

      Why it matters: understanding that difficult emotions and experiences are a natural part of life helps us build compassion—for ourselves and others. Recognizing this shared reality allows us to navigate challenges with greater resilience and empathy.

      Example: Imagine not being invited to a party that all your friends are talking about or failing a test you studied hard for. The sadness or frustration you feel is a form of Dukkha.

   2. **The Truth of the Cause of Suffering (Samudaya):**

      What it means: Suffering arises from desire and attachment. This can manifest as a craving for success, possessions, or recognition, which often leads to disappointment, frustration, or harm to us and others.

      Why it matters: Understanding our desires helps us see how they can lead to pain. By recognizing these emotions, we can learn to manage them more effectively and reduce the suffering they cause.

Example: Imagine scrolling through your social media feed - Facebook, Instagram, Tik Tok, etc. and seeing your friends post about their fabulous vacation. You might feel a desire for a similar experience leading to envy and be dissatisfied with your current situation. This attachment to an idealized lifestyle creates suffering.

3. **The Truth of the End of Suffering (Nirodha):**

    What it means: Suffering can end when we let go of cravings, attachments, or unhealthy desires. By releasing these, we can experience a sense of peace and freedom.

    Why it matters: This shows that there is hope to end suffering for those seeking to find peace and happiness.

    Example: When you feel grateful and happy with who you are and stop always trying to get others to like you, you feel calm and free from worrying about what others think.

4. **The Truth of the Path to the End of Suffering (Magga):**

    What it means: There is a way to overcome suffering and achieve enlightenment (Nirvana) by following the **Noble Eightfold Path**. This path offers guidelines for living ethically, training the mind, and developing wisdom to eliminate the causes of suffering.

The Noble Eightfold Path (Magga): The Noble Eightfold Path includes:

1. **Right Understanding (Samma Ditthi):** Recognizing the Four Noble Truths, that life has ups and downs. It's about knowing why we suffer and how to address it.

   Example: Constantly chasing material possessions can leave us feeling unfulfilled. By focusing on what truly matters, like relationships or personal growth we can make better choices that lead to lasting happiness.

2. **Right Intention (Samma Sankappa):** *"To do good, not to do evil and to purify the mind,"* that is the teaching of the Buddha.

   Example: Deciding to be kind to others, even when it's hard.

3. **Right Speech (Samma Vaca):** Words hold immense power shaping reality and relationships. Speak truthfully, kindly, and helpfully.

   Example: Avoid gossip and hurtful words and instead, speak in a way that uplifts others.

4. **Right Action (Samma Kammanta):** Acting in ways that are ethical and non-harmful to yourself and others.

   Example: Helping a friend in need rather than focusing solely on personal gain.

5. **Right Livelihood (Samma Ajiva):** Earning a living in a way that does not hurt and harm other people.

   Example: Choosing a job that doesn't take advantage of others or harm the environment.

6. **Right Effort (Samma Vayama):** Trying hard to do good things and stop bad habits.

   Example: Practicing patience and working to be better at something like being a good student, playing a musical instrument, or a sport instead of giving into frustration.

7. **Right Mindfulness (Samma Sati):** Being present and fully aware of your body, feelings, thoughts, and surroundings.

   Example: Paying attention to your thoughts and feelings, like noticing when you're feeling upset, then calming yourself down.

8. **Right Concentration (Samma Samadhi):** Focusing your mind through meditation or deep thinking to achieve calmness and clarity.

   Example: Setting aside time each day for focused breathing or meditation to calm your mind and reduce stress.

Why the Noble Eightfold Path matters: This is the Path towards enlightenment, to end suffering. It also gives us steps to follow to live a happier and peaceful life.

Challenges on the Path: The path knows it's hard to break old habits and let go of things you're attached to. It will take dedication, patience and continuous self-awareness. Just remember, every small step forward is progress, so keep on going!

The Five Precepts

Buddha's teachings are known as *Dhamma or Dharma*. He taught that wisdom, kindness, patience, generosity, and compassion were important virtues. As Theravada Buddhists, we live and uphold five moral precepts:

1. **Avoid killing living things:** This precept encourages respect for all forms of life, promoting compassion and non-violence.

   Example: Choosing not to participate in activities like trophy hunting or sport fishing where animals are killed for entertainment or display.

2. **Avoid taking what is not given:** This precept promotes honesty and respect for others' property.

   Example: Taking money from your mom's purse without her knowing.

3. **Avoid sexual misconduct:** This precept encourages respect and integrity in relationships.

   Example: Sending inappropriate messages to someone online while in a committed relationship, betraying trust and emotional commitment.

4. **Avoid lying or harmful speech:** This precept focuses on truthfulness and constructive communication.

   Example: Spreading rumors about your friends or posting false information online to harm someone's reputation.

5. **Consuming Alcohol or Using Drugs:** This precept emphasizes maintaining clarity of mind and avoiding behaviors that leads to harm.

   Example: You attended a party and drank too much. You became loud and aggressive. Your friends asked you to stop drinking, and you got into an argument because you were drunk and couldn't control your behavior.

The Triple Gem

In Buddhism, there is a community of support called the **Triple Gem** or **Three Jewels**. It consists of:

1. **Buddho:** Refers to the Buddha, the teacher who discovered the path to enlightenment. It also refers to the idea that every person has the potential for awakening within themselves.

2. **Dhammo:** Represents the Dharma, the teachings of the Buddha. These teachings guide us toward understanding truth and living a wise, compassionate life.

3. **Sangho:** Stands for the Sangha, the community that practices Buddhism. This includes monks, nuns, elders, and mentors who have achieved some level of awakening.

Buddho (Buddha teaches us), Dhammo (Buddha's Teaching guides us), and Sangho (the Community supports us). Together, they support the spiritual journey in Buddhism.

*Within the Sangha, monks and nuns are special teachers. They live in temples, study Buddhism and practice meditation full-time.

The Beginning of Theravada Buddhism in Laos

Present-day Laos is a small landlocked country with around 8 million people, located in Southeast Asia and surrounded by Thailand, Vietnam, China, Cambodia, and Myanmar. Around the year 1350, King Fa Ngum established the first Lao Kingdom, which was much larger in size than present-day Laos, including regions that are now in Northeast Thailand (Issan). King Fa Ngum brought Theravada Buddhist monks from Cambodia to teach Buddhism to his people. Since then, Theravada Buddhism has been the predominant religion in Laos. The direct ties between Laos and the Issan Region of Thailand are reflected in their shared language, heritage, culture, and food. The introduction of Theravada Buddhism by King Fa Ngum laid the foundation for the rich spiritual and cultural traditions that continue to thrive throughout Lao communities today.

Lao culture and Theravada Buddhism: What Festivals do we Celebrate?

Lao culture and community activities are deeply intertwined with Theravada Buddhism, which is not just a religion in Laos but a way of life. Throughout the year, various events serve as important traditional and spiritual milestones. Lao festivals and ceremonies are vibrant expressions of Lao culture and community.

At the temple, Lao people participate in the beautiful tradition of giving alms called Tahk Baht (the Alms Ceremony), hear sermons and participate in other merit making activities. These events provide opportunities for individuals to come together, uphold traditions, make merit, reflect on their spiritual journey, and celebrate the teachings of Buddha. Each festival, with its unique rituals and traditions, contributes to the rich tapestry of Theravada Buddhism.

In Laos, ceremonies and festivals are scheduled based on the Patitin Lao a Lunisolar Calendar. Lunisolar observes both the phases of the moon in the month and the earth's annual orbit around the sun.

In practicing communities outside of Laos, these festivals and celebrations are often staggered with different dates to avoid overlap and are held on weekends to accommodate work schedules. *Be sure to check with your nearby Lao Temple for their exact dates.*

Boun Makha Busa (Full Moon Ceremony):

When is it celebrated: This festival aligns with Boun Kao Jee and takes place during the third full moon of the Patitin Lao (Lao Lunisolar Calendar), typically in February. For communities abroad, it is often celebrated between February and March.

What it means: Boun Makha Busa is a significant religious festival that honors the time when 1,250 of the Buddha's first disciples spontaneously gathered to pay their respects to the Buddha. It marks the establishment of the Buddhist community, where they received a special sermon from the Buddha.

Rituals: A central ritual often includes **"Wien Tien,"** the candlelight procession ceremony, where followers walk clockwise three times around the prayer hall with candles, incense, and flowers in hand. This act symbolizes, respect, mindfulness, and commitment to the Buddha's teachings.

Boun Khao Jee (Devotion and Sticky Rice Offering Festival)

When is it celebrated: In Laos, Boun Khao Jee is held in the morning at the temple and coincides with Boun Makha Busa, typically in February. For communities abroad, it is usually celebrated between February and March.

What it means: For Theravada Buddhists, this special festival commemorates the Buddha's original teachings given to the monks. A unique tradition involves making a special "bread" from sticky rice, coated with egg, and then grilled. This bread is then offered to the monks in the morning as a symbolic act of devotion and gratitude.

Boun Khoun Khao (Rice Harvest Festival)

When is it celebrated: In Laos is celebrated usually in March. In communities abroad, this unique festival is typically held in December or January.

What it means: The Boun Khoun Khao (Rice Harvest Festival) is a celebration of the rice harvest, reflecting gratitude for agriculture and the land that sustains life in Laos. Villagers bring heaps of rice to be blessed by monks and donate it to the temple as an offering.

Key Traditions and Festivities:

- **Baci Ceremony:** A central part of the festival, the Baci ceremony involves village elders offering blessings for good health and future harvests. They tie cotton strings around attendees' wrists as a symbol of these blessings.
- **Feasting:** After the ceremony, villagers prepare a feast featuring local delicacies, such as fish, papaya salad, and Lao Sato (rice wine), made from the land's produce.
- **Entertainment**: The festival is filled with joy and energy as people come together to sing, dance, and enjoy traditional music, fostering a sense of community and celebration.

Have you heard of the traditional music genre called Peng Lum? Particularly from the Sithandone region called Lum Sithandone? It is one of Lao people's favorite!

Boun Phavet (Buddha's Life Stories and Spiritual Renewal Festival)

When it is celebrated: This major religious festival in Laos spans three days and three nights during the dry season in March. Abroad, the date varies with some temples waiting till the warmer months to celebrate. Be sure to check with your nearby temple for the exact date.

What it means: Boun Phavet is a significant Buddhist festival honoring the Jataka Tales—the life stories of the Buddha in his many incarnations before attaining enlightenment as Prince Siddhartha Gautama. This event celebrates the Buddha's journey through countless lifetimes, emphasizing endurance, sacrifice, and spiritual growth.

Key Traditions and Practices:

- **Jataka Recitation:** Monks take turns reading the entire scripture of the Buddha's previous lives over the course of three days and nights. This marathon reading symbolizes dedication and perseverance for both the monks and the devoted followers.
- **Spiritual Renewal:** The festival is considered an auspicious time for individuals to ordain as monks, nuns, or white-robed devotees (Mae Khao for women and Paw Khao for men). It's a period of deep reflection and commitment to the Buddhist path.
- **Seeking Guidance:** Many attendees use this time to consult elders or fortune tellers for advice on important life events, such as starting a business, planning a wedding, or making significant decisions. Guidance sought during this period is believed to carry heightened wisdom and blessings.
- **Community and Celebration:** Beyond its spiritual significance, the festival brings the community together in devotion and joy. It's a time for collective reflection, shared meals, and cultural bonding.

Boun Bee Mai Lao (Lao New Year)

When is it celebrated: Bee Mai Lao is a national holiday in Laos, officially celebrated over three days in mid-April during the hottest month of the year, to welcome the New Year. For Lao communities abroad, celebrations often occur between April and May, with dates staggered to avoid overlap between temples. These events are typically held on weekends to accommodate working schedules.

What it means: Lao New Year is a joyful and meaningful celebration for Lao people worldwide, marking the start of the Lao Patitin (Lao Lunisolar Calendar), which is based on both lunar phases and the sun's position. The three-day festival is filled with traditions that promote renewal, gratitude, and togetherness.

Key Traditions and Celebrations:

- **Day 1:** Farewell to the Old Year
  The first day is dedicated to preparing for the New Year. Families clean their homes, gather supplies for the festivities, and ceremonially wash Buddha images with scented water to purify and refresh them for the coming year.
- **Day 2:** Family Day
  This transitional day is unique as it is considered to belong neither to the old year nor the new. Families come together to honor elders, parents, and teachers by asking for forgiveness and showing love and respect.
- **Day 3:** Welcoming the New Year
  The final day is the highlight of the festival. It features the Baci Ceremony, a spiritual event in which participants tie cotton strings around each other's wrists while offering blessings of good luck, health, and prosperity for the coming year.

The Water Festival: One of the most exciting aspects of Bee Mai Lao is the Water Festival, where people joyfully spray, splash, and pour water on one another. Sometimes, they sprinkle baby powder as well.

This playful tradition symbolizes washing away the old year's misfortunes and welcoming a fresh start with happiness and renewal.

Boun Visakha Busa (Buddha Day Festival)

When is it celebrated: This major religious festival and national holiday is celebrated on the full moon day of the Lao Patitin (Lao Lunisolar Calendar) month of Visakha, in May. Abroad, it is also typically celebrated in May.

What it means: Boun Visakha Busa is a deeply significant Buddhist festival that commemorates three major events in the Buddha's life: his birth, enlightenment, and passing into Nirvana. Each of these events is believed to have occurred on the same day—the full moon in the middle of the month, of the sixth month. This festival highlights the importance of the middle path, a core principle of Buddhist teachings.

Before his passing, the Buddha shared his final words with his followers: *"All components in the world are impermanent. Nothing lasts forever. May you all strive with diligence and not be heedless."*

Key Rituals and Traditions: Wien Tien (Candlelight Procession): A central ritual involves the Wien Tien, or candlelight procession. Devotees walk clockwise three times around the temple's prayer hall, carrying candles, incense, and flowers as offerings. This act symbolizes respect, mindfulness, and devotion to the Buddha's teachings.

Boun Baang Fai (Rocket Festival)

When is it celebrated: In Laos, this festival is celebrated around May and June, aligning with the beginning of the rainy season and the eve of the planting season. Abroad, it is also typically held between May and June.

What it means: Boun Baang Fai is a culturally rich festival rooted in tradition and spirituality. While primarily a cultural event, it is also an occasion for merit-making, a key practice in Lao Buddhism. The festival is believed to invoke blessings from the heavens for sufficient rain, ensuring a bountiful rice harvest. Additionally, it is associated with prayers for fertility, seeking blessings for couples hoping to start a family.

Key Traditions and Highlights:

- **Morning Ceremony:** The day begins with a ceremonial offering and prayers, where participants ask for rain to nurture the fields and ensure agricultural prosperity.
- **Rocket Launching:** The centerpiece of the festival is the launching of homemade rockets. Traditionally, the rockets symbolize messages sent to the heavens to prompt rain. In modern times, this has evolved into a spirited competition where teams craft to display and launch colorful, high flying rockets adding excitement and community spirit to the event.

Boun Khao Phansa (Start of Buddhist Lent)

When is it celebrated: This major religious festival is also a national holiday in Laos observed on the full moon day of the eighth month, typically in July, commemorating the beginning of the rainy season. The Khao Phansa (Buddhist Lent) period runs until the full moon of the eleventh month in the Patitin Lao. Abroad, it is celebrated between July and August.

What it means: Boun Khao Phansa marks a three-month period where monks enter into the rainy season and stay within the temple grounds, dedicating their time to meditation and study. Many practicing Lao Theravada Buddhists, also dedicate themselves to studying and upholding the Four Noble Truths and the Noble Eightfold Paths. Additionally, some followers temporarily renounce specific cravings or desire such as - meat or other indulgences throughout the lent. This act of discipline symbolizes purification and commitment to self-improvement during this time.

Reflection: *What craving or habit will you give up during Lent to honor this meaningful tradition?*

Boun Haw Khao Padapdin (Spirits' Release and Earth Adornment Festival)

When is it celebrated: In Laos, this unique festival is observed in the middle of the rainy season, during the ninth month of the Patitin Lao calendar, typically in September. For Lao communities broad, it is celebrated between September and October.

What it means: Boun Haw Khao Padapdin is a sacred day dedicated to honoring and remembering deceased loved ones, ancestors, guardians, and even forgotten or family-less spirits. Falling on the day of the waning moon, this time is believed to mark the release of spirits, allowing them to roam freely. During the festival, Lao people make offerings to these spirits, which often include home-cooked meals, sticky rice, khao thom (steamed sticky rice wrapped in banana leaves), candy, fruits, and sometimes indulgent items like cigarettes or alcohol. These offerings symbolize love, respect, and gratitude for those who have passed.

The term "Padapdin" translates to "decorating the earth," signifying the act of remembrance and reverence. Along with honoring ancestors and spirits, the festival also pays homage to Mae Thoranee, the Goddess of Earth, who is believed to call on and pass these offerings on to the spirits, ensuring they are received.

Reflection: Boun Haw Khao Padapdin provides a meaningful opportunity to connect with the past, express gratitude for those who came before us, and honor the spiritual traditions that unify the living and the departed.

Boun Haw Khao Salak (Ancestor Remembrance Festival)

When is it celebrated: Boun Haw Khao Salak is observed on the full moon day of the tenth month in the Patitin (Lao Lunisolar Calendar), 15 days after Boun Haw Khao Padapdin (Spirits' Release and Earth Adornment Festival). In Laos, this festival typically occurs in late September or early October, while abroad, it is celebrated in October

What it means: This special festival offers Lao people a chance to make merit by honoring deceased loved ones, ancestors, and even forgotten spirits who have no family to remember them. It is a continuation of the reflective practices from Boun Haw Khao Padapdin, with an emphasis on generosity and remembrance.

During this time, people prepare "salak" baskets filled with items the departed might need or enjoy in the afterlife. These baskets often include staples such as instant noodles, rice, candy, soap, toothpaste, cigarettes, and even the favorite drinks of the deceased. The baskets can be personalized based on individual preferences or family traditions. In addition to these offerings, Lao people make gifts and monetary donations to honor spirits without living relatives, ensuring their peace and preventing disturbances to the living. The centerpiece of the ceremony involves monks who receive the salak baskets. The monks call out the names of the deceased, summoning their spirits to accept the offerings in the afterlife.

Tradition and Adaptation: In Laos, after the ceremony, the baskets are often redistributed to monks in a raffle-like system, as the number of monks sometimes exceeds the available baskets. Abroad, however, the smaller number of monks ensures that all participating monks receive a basket.

Reflection: Boun Haw Khao Salak emphasizes gratitude, respect for ancestors, and the importance of giving. It connects families and communities in a shared expression of love and care, ensuring that no spirit is forgotten and every soul is at peace.

Boun Auk Phansa (End of Buddhist Lent)

When is it celebrated: Boun Auk Phansa, a significant national holiday and religious festival, takes place on the full moon day in October. Abroad, the celebration is typically held between October and November.

What it means: The day begins with the practice of Tahk Baht (alms giving) at the temple, where devotees offer food and other essentials to monks, continuing tradition of merit-making. The most enchanting part of the festival, known as **Lai Heua Fai**, takes place in the evening. During this ritual, people release beautifully crafted floats into the river. These floats, often made from banana leaves and decorated with flowers, incense, and candles, are symbolic offerings. They are believed to carry away bad luck and negative energies, leaving participants with a sense of renewal and hope. The river comes alive with hundreds of colorful, glowing floats drifting gently under the night sky—a breathtaking sight that captures the spirit of joy, reflection, and unity. Families and communities come together to celebrate, strengthening their bonds and honoring tradition.

Boun Kathin (Kathin Merit Festival)

When is it celebrated: Boun Kathin is celebrated in November, immediately following Boun Auk Phansa (End of Lent), and lasts for a month until the next full moon. For Lao communities abroad, it is also observed in November, after Boun Auk Phansa celebrations.

What it means: Boun Kathin is a major religious ceremony where new robes and other essential items are offered to monks and nuns as they conclude their three-month period of meditation and study during the Buddhist Lent. This ceremony signifies the end of the monastic retreat, with the offerings symbolizing the community's support for the monks' spiritual practice.

The celebration often includes a Kathin parade, where followers walk in a clockwise direction around the prayer hall three times with their offerings, before presenting them to the monks and temple. It is widely believed that making Kathin offerings bestow the highest merit upon the donor, contributing to both spiritual growth and positive karma. Kathin donations can be made by individuals, families, organizations, or even entire villages, who collectively contribute to the ceremony and share in the merit. Many respected and affluent devotees strive for the honor of being the primary sponsor of the temple's Boun Kathin festival. This prestigious role is considered a once-in-a-lifetime opportunity and often requires a substantial financial contribution to help support the temple.

Boun Kathin is a time for large donations to be made to the temples, reflecting the community's devotion, generosity, and commitment to supporting the monastic community. It is a celebration of both spiritual and communal unity.

Boun That Luang (Golden Stupa Festival)

When is it celebrated: In Laos, this grand festival is a national holiday celebrated for three days, starting on the full moon of the twelfth month of the Patitin Lao Calendar, usually around November. Abroad, it is celebrated between November and December.

What it means: The That Luang Stupa is the most significant religious monument in Laos and is believed to house sacred relics of the Buddha, including his hair and breastbone. The Stupa is a powerful symbol of the Lao people and their nation. Every year, hundreds of monks and thousands of devotees from across Laos and the world make a pilgrimage to Vientiane, the capital of Laos, to celebrate this sacred festival.

At dawn, large crowds gather to offer alms to the monks who come from all parts of the country to pay tribute to the grand stupa. As part of the ceremony, Theravada Buddhists carry incense and candles, making offerings while walking three times in a clockwise direction around the stupa in reverence to the Buddha. This festival is one of Laos' most important cultural and spiritual events, uniting the Lao community in a powerful display of devotion and solidarity.

Would you like to take a trip to Laos one day and join in this meaningful celebration?

Boun Khao Kham (Renewal of Dedication Festival)

When is it Celebrated: In Laos it is observed in February. However, many temples abroad no longer practice this festival, and it has no fixed date. It's best to check with your local temple for the specific observance date.

What does it mean: This is a special spiritual purification time dedicated exclusively for monks. It is particularly significant for those who may have strayed in their practices, providing them with an opportunity for re-awakening.

During this period, monks engage in repentance and confession of their lapses to elder monks. The effort is to seek and renew commitment to their spiritual path. It's a deeply introspective time aimed at spiritual cleansing and rejuvenation, ensuring that they continue their journey with renewed dedication and clarity.

Unfortunately, outside of Laos, this practice is rarely observed as there are not enough monks in many temples to support one-another.

Does your local temple still uphold the tradition of Boun Khao Kham?

Basic Chanting and its Meaning

In Lao Theravada Buddhism, making merit is a fundamental practice, and chanting plays a central role in ceremonies. During these rituals, monks and temple elders guide the community in reciting chants in Pali, the ancient language of the Buddhist Pāli Canon Scriptures.

But what do these chants mean? To help you participate and deepen your understanding, here is a guide to the most common chants, transliterated and translated into English. These are widely practiced during various religious Lao festivals and ceremonies, serving as a bridge to connect you with their spiritual significance.

Pali Canon	English
Vandanâ	
Honoring and Paying Homage to the Triple Gem	
Start all ceremonies by respectfully and humbly taking the three Refuges. Bow down three times while quietly say:	
Buddho me natho	Buddha is my refuge. *(Bowing down the first time)*
Dhammo me natho	Buddha's teachings are my refuge. *(Bowing down the second time)*
Sangho me natho	The community of Buddhists is my refuge. *(Bowing down the third time)*

Seung Kataii

Pali Canon	English
	Paying Homage to Buddha *(Begin reciting)*
Imina sakārena taṃ buddhaṃ abhibhuchayāmi araham sammā sambuddho bhagavā Buddhaṃ bhagavantaṃ abhivādemi	I honor Buddha by bowing down. The Blessed One is worthy and rightly Self-Awakened. I bow down before the Awakened, Blessed One. *(Bow once when done)*
	Paying Homage to the Dhamma (Community)
Imina sakārena taṃ dhammaṃ abhibhu jayāmi svākkhāto bhagavatā dhammo dhammaṃ namassami	I honor the Dhamma by bowing down. The teachings were given by the Blessed One. I bow down before the Dhamma. (Bow once when done) *(Bow once when done)*
	Paying Homage to the Sangha (Community)
Imina sakārena taṃ sangkang abhibhu jayāmi supatipanno bhagavato sāvakasangho Sanghang namami	I honor the Sangha by bowing down. The community of practicing Buddhists has practiced well. I bow down before the Sangha. *(Bow once when done)*

Pali Canon	English
	Reciting Homage to the Blessed one (repeat three times).
Namô Tassa Bhagavatô Arahatô Sammâ-Sambuddhassa	Homage to the Blessed One, the Exalted One, the Fully Self-Awakened One
Namô Tassa Bhagavatô Arahatô Sammâ-Sambuddhassa	Homage to the Blessed One, the Exalted One, the Fully Self-Awakened One
Namô Tassa Bhagavatô Arahatô Sammâ-Sambuddhassa	Homage to the Blessed One, the Exalted One, the Fully Self-Awakened One

Ti-Sarana
The Three Refuges to Recite

Buddham Saranam Gacchâmi	I go to the Buddha as my refuge.
Dhammam Saranam Gacchâmi	I go to the Teachings as my Refuge.
Sangham Saranam Gacchâmi	I go to the Community as my Refuge
Dutiyampi Buddham Saranam Gacchâmi	For the second time I go to the Buddha as my Refuge.

Pali Canon			English
Dutiyampi Gacchâmi	Dhammam	Saranam	For the second time I go to the Teachings as my Refuge.
Dutiyampi Gacchâmi	Sangham	Saranam	For the second time I go to the Community as my Refuge.
Tatiyampi Gacchâmi	Buddham	Saranarn	For the third time I go to the Buddha as my Refuge.
Tatiyampi Gacchâmi	Dhammam	Saranam	For the third time I go to the Teachings as my Refuge.
Tatiyampi Gacchâmi	Sangham	Saranam	For the third time I go to the Community as my Refuge.

Buddha Vandana
Homage to the Buddha

Iti pi so Bhagavâ-Araham Sammâ-sambuddho. Vijjâ-carana sampanno Sugato Lokavidû Anuttarro Purisa-damma-sârathi Satthâ deva-manussânam Buddho Bhagavâti

Indeed, he is the Blessed One. He is the Holy One, fully self-awakened, with clear vision and virtuous conduct, sublime, the knower of the worlds, the incomparable leader of mankind, the teacher of gods and men, enlightened and blessed.

(Bow down and remain bowing till the end of the next verse)

Pali Canon	English
Kāyenavācā yavace tasāvā, Buddhe kukammaṁ pakataṁ mayāyaṁ, Buddho paṭiggaṇ hatuaccayantaṁ, Kāl'antare saṁvarituṁ va buddhe.	If I have done anything wrong to the Buddha through my actions, words, or thoughts, I ask for the Buddha's forgiveness. I promise to be more careful and respectful in the future.

Dhamma Vandana
Homage to the Teachings

Svâkkhato Bhagavatâ Dhammo Sanditthiko Akâliko Ehi-passiko Opanâyiko Paccattam veditabbo viññuhiti	The Buddha's teachings are perfectly created, meant to be experienced in the present. They are timeless, inviting everyone to explore them personally, and are relevant to those who observe them closely.

(Bow down and remain bowing till the end of the next verse)

Kāyenavācā yavace tasāvā, Dhamme kukammaṁ pakataṁ mayāyaṁ, Dhammo paṭiggaṇhatu accayantaṁ, Kāl'antare saṁvarituṁ va dhamme.	If I have done anything wrong to the teachings of Buddhism through my actions, words, or thoughts, I ask the Buddha for forgiveness. I promise to be more careful and respectful in the future.

| Pali Canon | English |

Sangha Vandana
Homage to the Community of Buddhist Followers

Supati-panno Bhagavato sâvaka sangho, Ujupati-panno Bhagavato sâvaka sangho. Ñâya-patipanno Bhagavato sâvaka sangho. Sâmici-patipanno Bhagavato sâvaka sangho Yadidam cattâri purisa yugâni attha-purisa-puggalâ Esa Bhagavato sâvaka sangho. Âhuneyyo, pâhu-neyyo, Dakkhineyyo, añjalikaraniyo, anuttaram puññakkhetam lokassâti

The community of the Buddha's followers who have practiced diligently, sincerely, methodically, and masterly in understanding and following the Four Noble Truths and the Noble Eightfold Path deserves great respect, gifts, kindness, and admiration. They are regarded as the greatest source of goodness and merit in the world.

(Bow down and remain bowing till the end of the next verse)

Kāyenavācā yavace tasāvā, Saṅghe kukammaṁ pakataṁ mayāyaṁ, Saṅgho paṭiggaṇ hatuaccayantaṁ, Kāl'antare saṁvaritum vasaṅghe

If I have done anything wrong to the Buddhist community, whether through my actions, words, or thoughts, I ask for their forgiveness. I promise to be more careful and respectful in the future.

Seung Kataii

Pali Canon

English

To Conclude the Honoring and Paying Homage to the Triple Gems, Recite:

Sādhu! Ukāsa, Vandāmi bhante cetiyaṁ, sabbaṁ sabbattha ṭhāne, supatiṭṭhitaṁ sārīraṅka-dhā tuṁ mahā-bodhiṁ buddha-rūpaṁ, sakkāraṁ Satā Kāyasā, Vāccasā, Mānasā Ceva vante-me te Tathāgate, sayane asāne thāne kamma ne cāpi sabbattā.

To well-being. I seek your permission, Venerable Sir, as we honor every stupa in every location, every relic of the Buddha's body, every Great Bodhi tree, and every Buddha image that is respected. Any impurity committed through body, speech, and mind; I wish to be absolved through praise of the Self-Awakened One. I aspire to receive the gift of liberation from karma as I bow down and honor him everywhere.

Ukāsa, Vandāmi bhante sabbaṁ apāradhaṁ khamata me, bhante maya kataṁ puññaṁ sāminā anumo thitāpaṁ, sāminā Kataṁ puññaṁ mayhaṁ, thātappaṁ. Sādhu! Sādhu! Sādhu! Anumothāmi.

I seek your permission, Venerable Sir. I ask for your forgiveness for any wrongs I have committed through the three channels of body, speech, and mind. As the owner of merit, may all beings rejoice in what has been offered. To Well-being! To Well-being! To Well-being! May they all share in the merit I have created.

When finished with this verse, respectfully and humbly take the

Pali Canon	English
	three Refuges. Bow down three times while quietly say:
Buddho me natho	Buddha is my refuge. *(Bowing down the first time)*
Dhammo me natho	Buddha's teachings is my refuge. *(Bowing down the second time)*
Sangho me natho	The community of Buddhists is my refuge. *(Bowing down the third time)*

Panca-Sila
Requesting Refuge in the Triple Gem and the Five Precepts

Mayaṁ bhante, vissuṁ-vissuṁ rakkhana taya. ti-saraṇena saha pañca sīlāni yācāma.	Venerable Sir, for purity and cleanliness of the Triple Gem, we request the Three Refuges and the Five Precepts.
Dutiyam-pi mayaṁ bhante, vissuṁ-vissuṁ rakkhana taya. ti-saraṇena saha pañca sīlāni yācāma.	Venerable Sir, a second time, for purity and cleanliness of the Triple Gem, we request the Three Refuges and the Five Precepts.

Pali Canon	English
Tatiyam-pi mayaṁ bhante, vissuṁ-vissuṁ rakkhana taya. ti-saraṇena saha pañca sīlāni yācāma.	Venerable Sir, a third time, for purity and cleanliness of the Triple Gem, we request the Three Refuges and the Five Precepts.

Receiving of the Triple Gem
Repeat and Recite after the Monk has finished each verse

Namô Tassa Bhagavatô Arahatô Sammâ-Sambuddhassa	Homage to the Blessed One, the Exalted One, the Fully Self-Awakened One
Namô Tassa Bhagavatô Arahatô Sammâ-Sambuddhassa	Homage to the Blessed One, the Exalted One, the Fully Self-Awakened One
Namô Tassa Bhagavatô Arahatô Sammâ-Sambuddhassa	Homage to the Blessed One, the Exalted One, the Fully Self-Awakened One
Buddham Saranam Gacchâmi.	I go to the Buddha as my refuge.
Dhammam Saranam Gacchâmi.	I go to the Teachings as my Refuge.
Sangham Saranam Gacchâmi.	I go to the Community as my Refuge.
Dutiyampi Buddham Saranam Gacchâmi.	For the second time I go to the Buddha as my Refuge.

Pali Canon			English
Dutiyampi Gacchâmi.	Dhammam	Saranam	For the second time I go to the Teachings as my Refuge.
Dutiyampi Gacchâmi.	Sangham	Saranam	For the second time I go to the Community as my Refuge.
Tatiyampi Gacchâmi.	Buddham	Saranarn	For the third time I go to the Buddha as my Refuge.
Tatiyampi Gacchâmi.	Dhammam	Saranam	For the third time I go to the Teachings as my Refuge.
Tatiyampi Gacchâmi.	Sangham	Saranam	For the third time I go to the Community as my Refuge.

Ti-saraṇa-gamanaṁ niṭṭhitaṁ

Do not recite (Monks Only):

Sadhu! Āma bhante

Buddhist followers Recite:
To Well-being, Venerable Sir
This ends the receiving of the Triple Gem

Receiving of the Five Precepts
Repeat and Recite after the Monk has finished each verse

Pânâtipâtâ Veramani Sikkhâpadam Samâdiyâmi.

I undertake the virtue to abstain from taking life.

Adinnâdânâ Veramani Sikkhâpadam Samâdiyâmi.

I undertake the virtue to abstain from stealing in taking what is not mine.

Pali Canon	English
Kâmesu Micchâcârâ Veramani Sikkhâpadam Samâdiyâmi.	I undertake the virtue to abstain from sexual misconduct.
Musâvâdâ Veramani Sikkhâpadam Samâdiyâmi.	I undertake the virtue to abstain from false speech in telling lies.
Surâ Mêraya Majja Pamâdatthânâ Verami Sikkhâpadam Samâdiyâmi	I undertake the virtue to abstain from taking any intoxicating alcohol and drugs that cause harm and lead to carelessness.

Conclude the receiving of the Triple Gem and Five Precepts by respectfully and humbly taking the three Refuges. Bow down three times while quietly say:

Buddho me natho	Buddha is my refuge
Dhammo me natho	Buddha's teachings are my refuge
Sangho me natho	The community of Buddhists is my refuge

Sabbī

Receiving Monk's Blessing. At every ceremony, Monks give a special blessing to community members.

Note: Members can also receive this blessing after every individual donation.

Yathā vārivahā pūrā Paripūrenti sāgaraṁ Evam-eva ito dinnaṁ Petānaṁ upakappati. Icchitaṁ	Just as rivers flowing with water fill the vast ocean, the blessings made here bring comfort and

Pali Canon

patthitaṁ tumhaṁ Khippameva samijjhatu Sabbe pūrentu saṅkappā, Cando paṇṇaraso yathā Maṇi jotiraso yathā.

Sabbītiyo vivajjantu Sabba-rogo vinassatu Mā te bhavatvantarāyo Sukhī dīgh'āyuko bhava. Abhivādana-sīlissa Niccaṁ vuḍḍhāpacāyino Cattāro dhammā vaḍḍhanti Āyu vaṇṇo sukhaṁ, balaṁ.

Sabba-roga-vinimutto Sabba-santāpa-vajjito Sabba-veram-atikkanto Nibbuto ca tuvaṁ bhava

English

support to the spirits of the deceased.

May all your wishes come true without delay, and may your dreams be fulfilled, shining brightly like the full moon and a radiant gem.

May all your troubles disappear. May every illness be healed. May you be protected from all dangers.

May you be happy and live a long life. For those who are respectful and honor the worthy, four things will always flourish: long life, beauty, happiness, and strength.

May you be free from sickness, safe from suffering, beyond all hatred, and free from desire.

Yād Ñām
Receiving Wish Fulfillment: The act of Pouring water in a cup/bowl.

Note: Once the ceremony has officially concluded, you can take your cup/bowl of water outside to water a nearby plant or tree.

Adāsi me akāsi me Ñāti-mittā sakhā ca me" Petānaṁ dakkhiṇaṁ dajjā Pubbe katam-anussaraṁ. Na hi

When we reflect on the good deeds of those who have passed away, it is important to make

runnaṁ vā soko vā Yā vaññā paridevanā Na taṁ petānam-atthāya Evaṁ tiṭṭhanti ñātayo. Ayañ-ca kho dakkhiṇā dinnā Saṅghamhi suppatiṭṭhitā Dīgha-rattaṁ hitāyassa Ṭhānaso upakappati. So ñāti-dhammo ca ayaṁ nidassito Petāna-pūjā ca katā uḷārā. Balañ-ca bhikkhūnam-anuppadinnaṁ Tumhehi puññaṁ pasutaṁ anappakanti.

merit in their memory. While tears and sorrow cannot help the deceased, offering donations to the temple in their name brings them immediate and lasting benefits. By doing so, we show respect to our relatives, honor the departed, and support the temple. The merit and good karma you generate from this act are profound and meaningful.

To Conclude all Theravada Buddhist Ceremonies, Recite:

Sādhu! Ukāsa, Vandāmi bhante cetiyaṁ, sabbaṁ sabbattha ṭhāne, supatiṭṭhitaṁ sārīraṅka-dhā tuṁ mahā-bodhiṁ buddha-rūpaṁ, sakkāraṁ Satā Kāyasā, Vāccasā, Mānasā Ceva vante-me te Tathāgate, sayane asāne thāne kamma ne cāpi sabbattā.

To well-being. I seek your permission, Venerable Sir, as we honor every stupa in every location, every relic of the Buddha's body, every Great Bodhi tree, and every Buddha image that is respected. Any impurity committed through body, speech, and mind; I wish to be absolved through praise of the Self-Awakened One. I aspire to recieve the gift of liberation from karma as I bow down and honor him everywhere.

Ukāsa, Vandāmi bhante sabbaṁ apāradhaṁ khamata me, bhante mayā kataṁ puññaṁ sāminā anumo thitāpaṁ, sāminā Kataṁ

I seek your permission, Venerable Sir. I ask for your forgiveness for any wrongs I have committed through the three channels of

puññaṁ Sādhu! Anumothāmi.	mayhaṁ, Sādhu!	thātappaṁ. Sādhu!	body, speech, and mind. As the owner of merit, may all beings rejoice in the offerings. To Well-being! To Well-being! To Well being! May they all share in the merit I have created.

To End all ceremony, respectfully and humbly take the three Refuges. Bow down three times while quietly say:

Buddho me natho   Buddha is my refuge
                           (Bowing down the first time)

Dhammo me natho   Buddha's teachings are my refuge
                           (Bow down the second time)

Sangho me natho   The community of Buddhists is my refuge
                           (Bow down the third time)

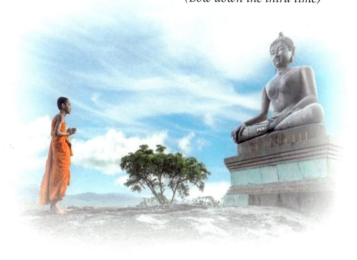

Incorporating Buddhism into Daily Life
Fundamental Practices for Individuals and Families

Mindful Living

- **Being Present:** Mindful living means paying attention to what you're doing right now. Whether you're breathing, eating, or walking. Focus on the present moment without letting your mind wander.

- **Daily Activities:** You can practice mindfulness in everyday tasks. For example, when you're eating, really notice the taste and texture of your food. When you're walking, feel each step you take.

- Putting your effort in following the **Four Noble Truths** and the **Noble Eightfold Path** (See pages 8 - 11).

The Four Noble Truths: These truths form the foundation of Buddhism:
1. The Truth of Suffering (Dukkha)
2. The Truth of the Cause of Suffering (Samudaya)
3. The Truth of the End of Suffering (Nirodha)
4. The Truth of the Path to the End of Suffering (Magga)

The Noble Eightfold Path
1. Right Understanding (Samma Ditthi)
2. Right Intention (Samma Sankappa)
3. Right Speech (Samma Vaca)
4. Right Action (Samma Kammanta)
5. Right Livelihood (Samma Ajiva)
6. Right Effort (Samm Vayama)
7. Right Mindfulness (Samma Sati)

8. Right Concentration (Samma Samadhi)

- **Ethical Living:** Mindful living also means following ethical rules of the **Five Precepts:**
  1. Avoid killing living things
  2. Avoid taking what is not given
  3. Avoid from sexual misconduct
  4. Avoid lying or harmful speech
  5. Avoid consuming alcohol or using drugs

- **Watching Your Thoughts:** Pay attention to your thoughts and feelings without getting caught up in them. Notice them, but don't let them control you.

- **Kindness and Compassion:** Practice being kind and caring towards yourself and others. Spend time thinking good thoughts about everyone, wishing them happiness and peace.

- **Learning and Growing:** By being mindful, you start to understand yourself and the world better. You see that everything changes, and nothing lasts forever. This helps you deal with life's ups and downs more calmly.

- **Morning and Evening Chanting in Learning:**
  Honoring and Paying Homage to the Triple Gem (see pages 26-33)

- **Meditation**
  Theravada Buddhist meditation practices are primarily divided into two main types: **Samathi (Calm)** Meditation and **Vipassana (Insight)** Meditation.

Samathi (Calm) Meditation

Objective: To develop a calm, concentrated, and tranquil mind.

Method:

- Find a quiet space and choose a comfortable place to sit.
- Posture: Sit in a comfortable position with your back straight. You can also sit cross-legged on the floor, on a chair with your feet flat on the ground or lying down with your arms down beside you.
- Start off by timing yourself for 5 minutes. Increase by a minute till you reach at least 30 minutes.
- Focus on the Breath: Close your eyes and bring your attention to your breath. Observe the sensation of the breath as it enters and leaves your nostrils or the rise and fall of your abdomen.
- Mental Noting: If your mind wanders, gently bring it back to your breath. You can use mental noting by silently saying "in" as you inhale and "out" as you exhale. Additionally, you can count to 8 while inhaling, then hold, and count to 12 while exhaling, then hold. The exact count depends on your ability to reach a calm and focused state, without feeling exhausted or struggling during your inhalation and exhalation. Keep repeating this process.
- Developing Concentration: Continue to focus on your breath, allowing your mind to become more concentrated and calmer. This practice helps to develop one-pointedness of mind.

Vipassana (Insight) Meditation (Try practicing after being comfortable with Samathi Meditation)

Objective: To gain insight into the true nature of reality, particularly the impermanence, suffering, and non-self-aspects of existence.

Method:

- Preparation: Begin with 5 minutes of Samathi meditation to calm the mind.
- Observation: Shift your focus from the breath to observing bodily sensations, thoughts, and emotions as they arise and pass away.
- Mental Noting: Use mental noting to label your experiences, such as "thinking," "feeling," "itching," or "hearing." This helps to maintain awareness and prevent identification with the experiences.
- Non-Reactivity: Observe each experience without reacting to it. Simply note it and let it go, recognizing its impermanent nature.
- Insight Development: Through continuous observation, you begin to see the impermanent, unsatisfactory, and self-nature of all phenomena. This leads to deeper understanding and wisdom.

Combined Practice:

Some practitioners combine both Samathi and Vipassana meditation, starting with calm meditation to stabilize the mind then transitioning to insight meditation to develop deeper understanding. These meditation practices are integral to the spiritual development of Theravada Buddhists, helping them cultivate mindfulness, concentration, and insight on their path to enlightenment.

PRONUNCIATION OF PĀLĪ-ENGLISH TEXT

PĀLĪ-ENGLISH PRONUNCIATION

Consonance - Similar to English however certain letters have either an aspirated sound or unaspirated sound. Also, there are some letters that sound different than how it would be pronounced in English. Here is a tabled list of Consonants aspirated, unaspirated, and special sound.

aspirated	example	Pālī-English Example	Phonetic Sound
BH & PH	UPHOLSTERY	Bhagavato	**Puht** ka-wa doe
D & DH & TH	THOMAS	Dhammaṁ	**Thum** mung
GH & KH	KAREN	Svākkhāto	Suh-wuh **Khar** doe

un-aspirated	example		
B & P	SPOT	Buddhaṁ	**Bput** tongue
K & G	SKIN	Bhagavā	Pot **ka**-wah
T	STOP	Tam-ahaṁ	**Dtumb** Uh-Hung

special	Example		
C	JAVELIN	Sāmīci	Sah mee **Je**
J & CH	XEROX or SHY	Jāti-pi	**Shar** dtee bpe
V	WELCOME	Veditabbo	**Way** Te Dtup bpow
Ñ	CANYON	viññūhi	Wean-**You** Heat
ṁ & ṅ	SING	saraṇaṁ	Suh-rut **nung**
ṭ or ṇ	Shortens the vowel and connects to next word	aṭṭha & chabbaṇṇa	Uht-Thuht & Shup pun-nuh

Here is a tabled list of **Vowels** (How Sanskrit-English is written?)

A	O or AH	E	U	I	AY
father (uh)	gopher	they	gluten	pink	Eye
ā	—	—	ū	ī	—
farther (Ahhh)	—	—	OOzing	machine	—

Glossary of Terms

Common Buddhist Terms and Their Meanings

1. **Anatta:** The concept of no-self; the belief that there is no permanent, unchanging self.
2. **Arahant:** A person who has achieved enlightenment and liberation from samsara.
3. **Buddha:** Siddhartha Gautama, the founder of Buddhism, who attained enlightenment and taught the path to end suffering. Additionally, Buddha literally translates into 'the awakened one.' The term "Budh" means awakened, and "Buddh-a" means one who woke up from illusion.
4. **Dukkha:** The truth of suffering; the first of the Four Noble Truths.
5. **Enlightenment:** The state of complete understanding and freedom from suffering, also known as Nirvana.
6. **Five Precepts:** The basic ethical guidelines for Buddhist, which prohibit killing living things, taking what is not given, sexual misconduct, lying, and using drugs and alcohol.
7. **Karma:** The law of cause and effect, where actions have consequences that shape future experiences - you create it and experience it.
8. **Khao thom:** Steamed sticky rice with various fillings wrapped in banana leaves. The most popular of which is the Khao Thom with banana filling
9. **Impermanence:** The belief that everything is transient and constantly changing.
10. **Magga:** the truth of the path to end of suffering, which is the Noble Eightfold Path; the fourth of the Four Noble Truths.
11. **Merit:** is a beneficial force that results from good deeds. It is one of the most important practices in Buddhism.
12. **Nirodha:** The truth of the end of suffering, which is achieved by letting go of cravings; the third of the Four Noble Truths.

13. **Nirvana:** The ultimate goal of liberation from the cycle of rebirth.
14. **Noble Eightfold Path:** The path to enlightenment, consisting of Right Understanding, Right Intention, Right Speech, Right Action, Right Livelihood, Right Effort, Right Mindfulness, and Right Concentration.
15. **Pali Canon:** A collection of ancient scriptures that are considered the most authentic record of the Buddha's teachings.
16. **Patitin** (Calendar): Is a Buddhist Calendar taking into account both the moon's phases and the sun's position in the sky.
17. **Samsara:** The cycle of birth, death, and rebirth.
18. **Samudaya:** The truth of the cause of suffering, which is craving or desire; the second of the Four Noble Truths
19. **Theravada Buddhism:** One of the oldest forms of Buddhism, emphasizing the teachings of the Buddha as preserved in the Pali Canon.

FESTIVAL CALENDAR

Month	Festival	When in Laos	When abroad
February to March	Boun Makha Busa (Full Moon Festival)	Third full moon of the Patitin Lao typically in February	Between February and March
February	Boun Khao Jee (Devotion and Sticky Rice Offering Festival)	Third full moon of the Patitin Lao typically in February	Between February and March
March	Boun Khoun Khao (Rice Harvest Festival)	Typically, in March	December or January
March	Boun Phavet (Buddha's Life Stories and Spiritual Renewal Festival)	Three days and nights during the dry season in March	No fixed date, check with nearby temple (often in warmer months)
April	Boun Bee Mai Lao (Lao New Year)	Officially celebrated over three days in mid-April	Between April and May on the weekend. Check with nearby temple
May	Boun Visakha Busa (Buddha Day Festival)	Typically, in May on the Full moon day of Visakha	Typically, celebrated in May
May to June	Boun Baang Fai (Rocket Festival)	Around May and June, aligning with the beginning of the rainy season	Between May and June

Month	Festival	When in Laos	When abroad
July	Boun Khao Phansa (Start of Buddhist Lent)	In July, Full moon day of the eighth month, celebrating the beginning of the rainy season	Between July and August
September	Boun Haw Khao Padapdin (Spirit's Release and Earth Adornment Festival)	Typically, September. Observed in the middle of the rainy season, ninth month of the Patitin Lao calendar	Between September and October
September to October	Boun Haw Khao Salak (Ancestor Remembrance Festival)	Full moon day of the tenth month in the Patitin Lao usually 15 days after Boun Haw Khao Padapdin in September or October	Late September or early October
October	Boun Auk Phansa (End of Buddhist Lent)	Full moon day in October	Between October and November
November	Boun Kathin (Kathin Merit Festival)	Celebrated in November, immediately following Boun Auk Phansa	November after Boun Auk Phansa
November to December	Boun That Luang (Golden Stupa Festival)	Grand festival starting on the full moon of the twelfth month of the Patitin Lao Calendar typically in November	Between November and December
February	Boun Khao Kham (Renewal of Dedication Festival)	Practiced in February	No fixed date, check with nearby temple

References

Banlusak, Phramaha Singthong and Phramaha Sidthisak Kaybounthome. *Morning and Evening Chanting*, n.p., 2013

Manivong, Bounheung. *The 227 Rules of Monks (Bhikkus)*, n.p., 2013

"Home." *Access to Insight*, n.d., https://accesstoinsight.org/. Accessed 24 July 2024.

"Home." *Wat Lao Veluwanh*, n.d., https://www.watlao-veluwanh.org/home. Accessed 24 June 2024.

"Home." *Dhamma Talks*, n.d., https://www.dhammatalks.org/. Accessed 24 June 2024.

"Tourism Laos. "Festivals." Tourism Laos, https://www.tourismlaos.org/welcome/buddhism-and-belief/festivals/. Accessed 1 November 2024."

"Sonasia Holiday. "Laos Festivals." Sonasia Holiday, https://sonasiaholiday.com/sonabee/laos-festivals Accessed 1 November 2024."

"Pali Chanting in Theravada Buddhist Tradition." *BuddhaNet*, n.d., http://buddhanet.net/pali_chant.htm. Accessed 24 July 2024.

"Pali Chanting in the Theravada Buddhist Tradition Homage to ..." *Addhana Magga*, n.d., https://www.addhanamagga.uk/wp-content/uploads/. Accessed 25 June 2024.

"Who are Monastics? Who are Lay People?" *Wat Lao Veluwanh*, n.d., https://www.mahamevnawawinnipeg.org/who-are-monastics-who-are-lay-people.html. Accessed 25 June 2024.

O'Brien, Barbara. "Taking Refuge: Becoming a Buddhist." *Learn Religions*, Dotdash Meredith, 25 July 2018, https://www.learnreligions.com/taking-refuge-becoming-a buddhist-450056. Accessed 25 June 2024.

Afterword

In Buddhism, faith is not about blind acceptance, but about personal exploration and self-discovery of the truths taught by the Buddha. This guide is designed as a practical resource for English-speaking individuals, offering a concise introduction to Theravada Buddhism, the predominant religion practiced by most Lao people worldwide.

Beyond explaining the core beliefs and practices of Theravada Buddhism, this guide seeks to encourage meaningful conversations and discussions within families. By exploring these traditions together, families can strengthen their cultural bonds, deepen their understanding of shared heritage, and engage in thoughtful dialogue about their beliefs and values.

As a former Theravada Buddhist monk and a dedicated practitioner, I have drawn from a rich reservoir of knowledge and experience. Every effort has been made to provide information to the best of my ability, informed by thorough research, oral interviews with monks and practitioners. It is my sincere hope that this work serves as a meaningful resource for those seeking insight into the teachings and practices of Theravada Buddhism.

Acknowledgement

I dedicate this guide to those who have profoundly influenced my journey as a devout Theravada Buddhist. Your unwavering support has shaped my spiritual path and enriched my life as a man of service. Your dedication to our small Lao communities abroad ensures that the traditions and wisdom of Theravada Buddhism thrive and inspire future generations. Beyond religious guidance, you tirelessly work to preserve our culture and traditions as our community continues to widen and prosper outside of Laos.

I extend my heartfelt gratitude, and I honor:

- Venerable Phramaha Singthong Banlusak
- Venerable Phramaha Sam Khamphoukeo
- Venerable Phramaha Sounthone Inthirath
- Venerable Phramaha Bouasing Sisoubahns
- Maha Phaisane Chantaphone
- Maha Bounheuang Manivong
- Maha Khamphoui Sisavatdy
- Mrs. Thongsavanh Sananikone Sisavatdy Khonekham
- To My Dearest Family, Thank You for your Eternal Love and Support – I Love You

Lastly, I offer my deepest reverence to the Triple Gem - the Buddha, the Dhamma, and the Sangha - my eternal refuges.

Khop Jai (Thank You)

- Seung Kataii

Made in the USA
Columbia, SC
23 April 2025